THUMP

THE FIRST BUNDRED DAYS

TIMOTHY LIM & MARK PELLEGRINI

with **BRETT R. SMITH**

A POST HILL PRESS BOOK

Thump:
The First Bundred Days
© 2017 by Timothy Lim, Mark Pellegrini, and Brett R. Smith
All Rights Reserved

ISBN: 978-1-68261-522-5
ISBN (eBook): 978-1-68261-430-3

Post Hill Press
New York • Nashville
posthillpress.com

Published in the United States of America

To Gus, Hugo, Mr.Bennett,
Thatcher, and Moneypenny:
The Silent Majority
Stands with Thump.
- Tim

To Goblin the Cat:
Making the Apartment
Great Again.
- Mark

And to Marlon Bundo Pence,
the First Rabbit of the United States:
Truly a Bun of the People.

"He understands that the Media has to chase rabbits, so he gives them rabbits to chase: because if he doesn't give them rabbits to chase, they'll invent a rabbit."

~ Newt Gingrich, December 26, 2016

THIS YUUUUUGE BOOK BELONGS TO:

_____

SO TRUE.

THUMP
PENCE
THE FIRST BUNDRED DAYS
2016

ILLUSTRATED BY TIMOTHY LIM
WRITTEN BY MARK PELLEGRINI
with BRETT R. SMITH, EDITOR & CREATIVE DIRECTOR
ADDITIONAL EDITING by COLIN MADINE

Starring
Mr. Thump

and Marlon
Bundo Pence

ACT I

Mr. Thump was born in the US of A
And prospered thanks to the American Way.

As Thump's businesses flourished and his investments rose,
He wanted to give back to his country and to those

Who supported him throughout the thick and the thin.
Thump would fight for his country; he'd fight and he'd win!

He declared through the wilderness, oppressed for eight long years,
That he would be their next President through blood, sweat and tears!

He'd make America great, like it had been before,
And he'd bring back the jobs that had been taken offshore.

He'd keep America safe from those who meant to do harm
By implementing common sense as a safety alarm.

The Establishment laughed, but his movement believed
That Thump's campaign promises could all be achieved.

Some thought that Thump was a joke, but the joke was on them
When all the funny little frogs rallied around him.

As the Primaries began, Thump's enemies conspired
But the voters told them without stuttering: "**You're FIRED!**"

The cheaters and the cowards and the dynasty brats
Were cast into the trash or sent scurrying like rats.

Because Thump did one thing that they could not do correctly:
Just speak to the citizens and address them directly.

★ ★ ★ ★ ★

Thump went down the rabbit hole as the camera flashes lit
And he announced that his run for President was legit.

THE HOPPINGTON POST

JUNE 16, 2015

THUMP ANNOUNCES PRESIDENTIAL RUN

"NOBODY BUILDS WALLS BETTER THAN ME"

Long before the rabbit hole, a dog gave Thump a prediction:
He'd win the White House and serve the Democrats an eviction.

Thump found friends in strange places and in all shapes and sizes,
Such as the frogs that croaked "KEK!" They were full of surprises!

One of Thump's first adversaries was a man who loved guac.
Thump toppled his dynasty and gave the experts a shock!

The Establishment Rhinos blockaded Thump out of fear
Until Thump's buddy Doc arrived to help keep the path clear.

Teddy and Rubiobot whined, but their cries went ignored
When the train conductor shouted to his friends: "ALL ABOARD!"

With the votes counted, Thump had won in a field of sixteen!
He'd been chosen to take on the Democrats' Crooked Queen.

Thump was joined by his V.P. pick, Marlon Bundo Pence,
And they rallied as the last race was soon to commence.

ACT II

Now the time had come for the General Election
Where citizens would make their ultimate selection.

The Mainstream Media didn't like Thump at all
And joined with his foes to orchestrate his downfall.

The media kings had decided well in advance
Who would be President and wouldn't leave it to chance.

So Thump was pitted against a cruel adversary
Who believed she could triumph through means monetary.

Known as The Crooked One, villains financed her campaign
Even though it was clear that she was sick in the brain.

And then there were the Rhinos, the old Establishment guard,
Who were blocking Thump and his movement, and blocking it hard!

Thump and Pence were attacked on every side, every day,
But stood their ground through it all and did things their own way.

The forgotten voters saw through The Crooked One's lies,
So she called them "deplorables" with hate in her eyes.

And then the Mainstream Media, which had been bought and paid,
Were being challenged by the voices of those unafraid.

Through it all, Thump persevered as he rallied the nation
And his campaign concluded with a YUGE celebration!

The Crooked fiend was vanquished! The election was won!
Thump's next stop was the White House. His work had just begun...

★ ★ ★ ★ ★

When the Mainstream Media refused to cover Thump squarely,
A little twittering bird helped him reach the masses fairly.

TWEET

Donald J. Thump
@POTUSThump

Happy #CincoDeMayo! The best taco bowls are made in Thump Tower Grill. I love Hispanics!

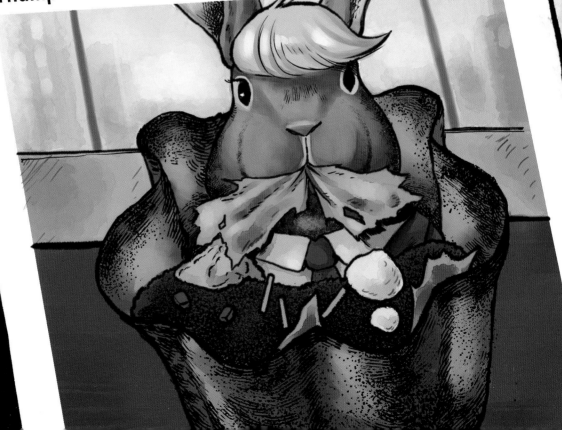

If she couldn't break Thump's spirit, the Crooked One believed
She'd cook his spirit instead, but her scheme wasn't achieved.

Unlike the Crooked One, Thump wasn't in it for the fame.
Making America great was his solitary aim.

The Crooked One saw Thump's friends, wonderful and adorable
Secretly she said they were a "basket of deplorables."

Les Déplorabuns

The Rhinos said no rabbits beyond the velvet rope.
Ditching the old Establishment was Thump's only hope.

Protesters, thugs & bullies attacked Thump's friends when they met.
Bikers formed a "wall of fluff" to keep them safe from the threat.

Thump promised to the miners, forced to abandon their hole,
That greatness could be achieved thanks to American coal.

The Media hated Thump and he was constantly wronged,
But he knew exactly where their "journalism" belonged...

Thump was caught talking of grabbing all things pusillanimous:
Protesters even made pink hats: their ire was unanimous.

When things looked dicey, Thump was ditched by Mister McTurtle
Who was left speechless as Thump made it over the hurdle.

...VERSY OVER LEAKED BUSH TAPE

...p | (R) Presidential Candidate

DISAVOWING THUMP
SENATE MAJORITY LEADER HIDES IN HIS SHELL

LOWEST LABOR PARTICIPATIO
SINCE 1970'S

95 MILLION AMERICANS OUT O
THE LABOR FORCE

WORST RECOVERY SINCE 1940

LOWEST HOME OWNERSHIP
RATE IN 51 YEARS

ALMOST 13 MILLION MORE
AMERICANS ON FOOD STAMPS

VER 43 MILLION LIVING IN
TY

MANATEE

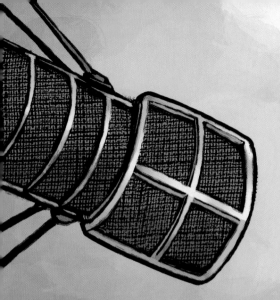

It was the goal of the Media: Thump's movement it would crush
But he had good friends in Mr. Manatee and Mr. Thrush.

While a few states went blue, many more of them turned red.
The game was approaching the end: Thump Fever had spread!

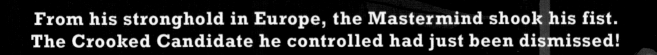

From his stronghold in Europe, the Mastermind shook his fist.
The Crooked Candidate he controlled had just been dismissed!

ACT III

Inauguration Day came and Thump held out his paw,
Swearing with pride he would uphold Order and the Law.

Crowds gathered in the swamp known as Washington, D.C.
And chanted together in true solidarity.

The Establishment, defeated, were not out of tricks
And vowed to obstruct him in the world of politics.

They enjoyed their lives in the swamp and did not want it drained.
It was of utmost importance their leisure was maintained!

They fought Thump and they fought Pence, but each fight was a loss.
All too late they realized who was *really* the Boss.

But Thump had his own bosses and promises to keep
And he had a whole lot to do before he could sleep.

The Establishment fat-cats were promptly given the boot
And replaced by a new team that was far more resolute.

Together with Thump, they would bring America back
To the heights it once soared at before things went offtrack.

As for all of the snowflakes who didn't give Thump their vote,
They were bawling and complaining until sore in the throat.

But despite all of their crying, protesting and screeching,
No one cared anymore about their self-absorbed preaching.

Because their country was emerging from a long, dark slump.
America was great again, thanks to **President Thump**.

★ ★ ★ ★ ★

THUMP "THANK YOU" VICTORY TOUR

Thump | (R) President - Elect

Thump quenched his thirst with hearty gulps of liberal tears
From a reservoir that stayed full for his White House years.

As the Crooked One retreated, she left snowflakes behind
And each delicate one melted as their season declined.

"Good fences make good neighbors," which is a very old saying.
Thump vowed to build a wall and that the neighbors would be paying.

The Donkeys couldn't do much, but they knew how to whine.
A shame no one would listen to a pouty equine.

Thump teamed-up with his friend Mad Dog, a ferocious Marine,
To protect America from threats both known and unseen.

Then came Thump's buddy, T-Rex, a fan of fossil fuels.
He'd show the world why American energy rules!

With one turn of the crank, Thump set the D.C. Swamp to drain,
Exposing the Bottom-Feeders, who had much to explain!

With a paw on the Lincoln Bible and a paw in the air,
Thump pledged to Make America Great Again: his most solemn prayer.

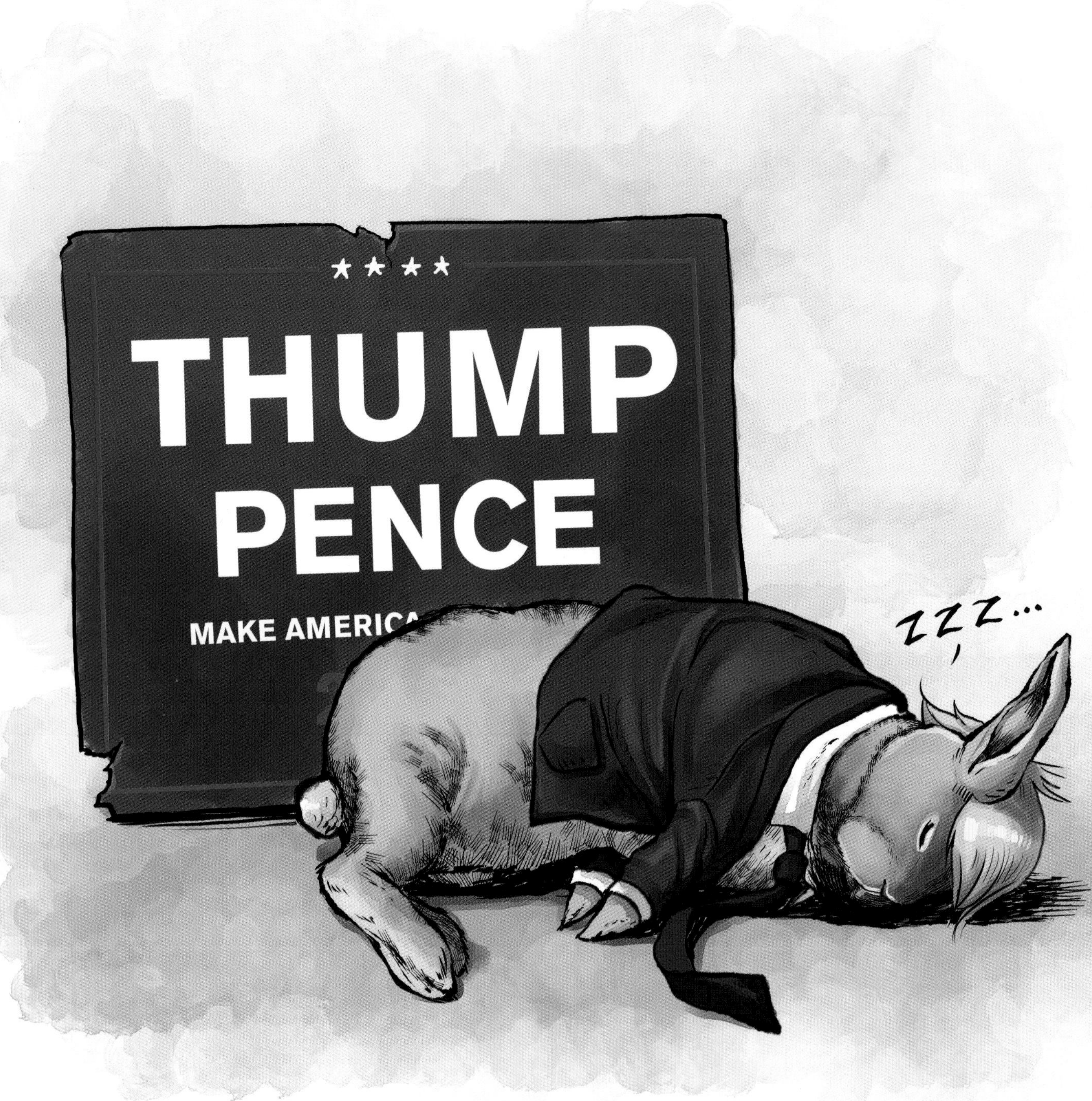
★★★★
THUMP
PENCE
MAKE AMERICA
ZZZ...

The art of Timothy Lim has been featured on licensed merchandise for companies such as Marvel, Lucasfilm, and Hasbro. He has contributed cover art for a variety of books by IDW, including Back to the Future, TMNT Universe, Street Figther X GI Joe, and Optimus Prime. You can also see his art in UDON's series of "Tribute" artbooks and Street Fighter Vs. Darkstalkers. He currently resides between Arkansas and Texas with his wife & 5 rabbits.

Mark Pellegrini is a creative consultant and writer for NINJAINK, LLC, and his collaborations with Timothy Lim have been published by IDW and UDON studios. As a freelance featured writer, his articles and creative works have been published by such websites as Adventures in Poor Taste, Comics Alliance, Ain't It Cool News, and io9. You can find more of his writing at TMNT Entity. He currently resides in the red state of Arkansas with his cat.

Brett R. Smith is a professional illustrator working in the graphic novel industry as an editor, creatve director, colorist, and graphic designer. He holds a B.F.A. in Animation. Smith has contributed to multiple premier properties and licenses including The Avengers, Batman, Superman, GI Joe, Wolverine, Suicide Squad, Guardians of the Galaxy, and Hulk. Smith was a co-adapter, editor and creative director for the New York Times #1 best seller, Clinton Cash: A Graphic Novel.